The Pilgrims' First Thanksgiving

BY ANN McGOVERN

ILLUSTRATED BY ELROY FREEM

SCHOLASTIC INC.

New York Toronto London Auckland Sydney
Mexico City New Delhi Hong Kong Buenos Aires

To dear friends
who welcome me
to their feasts.

A.M.

Text copyright © 1973 by Ann McGovern. Illustrations copyright © 1993 by Mark Teague.

12 11 10 9 8 7 6 5 4 3 2 1   5 6 7 8 9/0

Printed in Singapore   46

This edition created exclusively for Barnes & Noble, Inc.

2005 Barnes & Noble Books

ISBN 0-7607-9587-8

This edition first printing, October 2005

A long time ago, some men and women, boys and girls, two dogs and a cat sailed on a ship across the sea.

They left their old country because they could not pray the way they wanted. The people were called Pilgrims. The ship was called the *Mayflower*.

The *Mayflower* was as big as two trucks. But it was not big enough. The Pilgrims and sailors crowded together to sleep. They crowded together to eat. The children had no room to run around. They had no toys. They had to leave most things behind.

The Pilgrim children hated the food on the ship. But they had to eat it. There was nothing else. Nothing but the same old salted beef or fish. Nothing but the hard, dry biscuits. A little bite of cheese. A little bit of butter.

After a while, the food turned bad. There was not enough water for drinking or washing.

The children couldn't sleep in warm, cozy beds. They slept
on the hard, cold floor of the ship. They slept in the same
clothes they wore every day. Their clothes got torn and dirty
and smelly.

Day by day, things got worse.

Storms came. The wind blew hard. The waves tossed the ship about. The *Mayflower* rolled and creaked in the stormy sea. The rain soaked the ship. The rain poured on the Pilgrims. They were cold and wet.

Many of the Pilgrims got sick. Would this terrible voyage ever end? They prayed for the day they would see land.

They had sailed away in warm September. Now it was cold November. They had been on the *Mayflower* for two months and three days. The next day they saw land.

They were very happy. But they were scared, too. What
kind of land was this? There were no houses. No stores.
No people to meet them. Only an empty, white, sandy beach
with trees and bushes behind it.

Oh, but it was good to be on land again. The Pilgrim
children ran up and down the beach, feeling the sand and the
land beneath their feet.

WINTER

Winter was coming. The Pilgrims had to find a safe place for all of them to live.

Every day a group of Pilgrims searched the wild countryside. At last they came to a place with running brooks and rivers, and good land for planting. It was a good place to build their town. They named it Plymouth.

They wanted a street to go from the shore to the top of the hill. They wanted a fort on the top of the hill. They wanted houses on both sides of the street. They would have to make everything themselves.

It would take a long, long time to finish building Plymouth. In the meantime, they would have to sleep on the *Mayflower*.

The first winter in Plymouth was terrible for the Pilgrims.
They could not finish building their homes before the snow
fell. They could not find enough food in the forests.

The Pilgrims worked as hard as they could. But they were hungry and cold and weak. That winter, many of the Pilgrims got sick. Many of the Pilgrims died.

SPRING

At last the snows began to melt. Spring was coming.

There was so much work to be done. The Pilgrims worked every day but Sunday. Sunday was the time to think about God. They prayed and sang and listened to long sermons.

Every day but Sunday, the Pilgrims worked very hard. They worked making houses. They made their houses from bark and branches. They made the roofs from straw and vines. Each house had only one room and a small space upstairs.

The house got cold when the wind blew in through the holes in the wall. The house got wet when the rain dripped down through the holes in the roof.

The only heat came from the fire in the fireplace. Sometimes sparks flew up the chimney and set the straw roof on fire. Then everybody ran outside to put the fire out.

The Pilgrims worked making furniture for the houses. They didn't make much — just some stools and benches and beds. To save space, the children's beds were pushed under the big bed during the day.

People used the benches for tables, or put their plates on their knees. There were no glasses. So the Pilgrims drank out of mugs made of leather or wood. Their plates and bowls were wooden, too. There were no forks. The Pilgrims used shells for spoons.

The only iron things in the house were the iron pots and pans. One big iron pot was used for boiling the stew, or making the candles, or making the soap.

The Pilgrims worked planting their gardens. Each family planted a small garden with seeds brought over on the *Mayflower*.

The Pilgrims made a good friend who helped them. His name was Squanto. Squanto was one of the people who had lived near Plymouth years before the white men came. He taught the Pilgrims everything about the land he knew so well.

He took the Pilgrims to the rivers and showed them where the fish swam, and the best ways to catch them. He took the Pilgrims to the forest and showed them where to find the deer and turkey, and how to hunt them. He showed the Pilgrims where the wild plants grew — the ones that were good to eat and the ones that were good for making medicines. And he showed the Pilgrims the best way to plant corn.

Squanto lived with the Pilgrims for the rest of his life. The Pilgrim children loved him and followed him everywhere. He taught them stories and Indian words. He taught them how to make traps and how to skin animals. The children learned many things from Squanto.

There was no real school that first year in Plymouth. The children learned reading and writing from the Pilgrims who knew how.

The children learned other things at Plymouth. They learned good manners. At mealtime, good manners meant eating standing up, and eating with their hats on, and not speaking unless a grown-up spoke to them first.

The Pilgrim children learned to work hard — just as hard as the grown-ups. They had to watch the cornfield and shoo away birds and animals. They had to make the big roasts and turkeys.

They sat near the hot fire and turned the stick that turned the roast. That job took most of the day.

They had other special jobs, too. They had to make mattresses for sleeping. They stuffed pine needles or rags or feathers into big bags. They walked miles to gather grasses for the roofs of the houses. They dug clams out of the mud and picked black mussels from the rocks in the water.

Every day they cooked and they served and they helped with the washing and the making of soap and the making of candles.

Everyone worked harder than they ever worked before. They worked from morning until night. But no one wanted to give up and go back. And when the *Mayflower* sailed back to England in April, there was not a single Pilgrim on board.

SUMMER

By summer, seven houses were finished and more were being built. The gardens were bursting with vegetables. The corn was growing tall.

The Pilgrims met more friendly Indians who lived nearby. Their new friends showed the children where to find nuts and where the wild fruit grew. The Pilgrims and the Indians made flour, baked corn bread, and ate together.

Summer was the best time for the Pilgrims. There was plenty for all to eat. And there would be plenty when winter came. No one would go hungry. The Pilgrims wanted to celebrate.

THANKSGIVING

The first Thanksgiving in America lasted three whole days. From the forests the Pilgrims got wild turkeys, geese, and ducks. The Indians got five deer. From the waters they caught lobsters, clams, oysters, and pounds of fish.

From the gardens they gathered cucumbers, carrots and cabbages, turnips and radishes, onions and beets. Corn was cooked in many ways. There was popcorn, too! There were wild fruits for dessert. Thanksgiving was a time for eating and for sharing.

All of the Pilgrims took part. So did their Indian friends.
Ninety Indians came. There were more Indians than Pilgrims.

The men and the boys played games and had jumping and running and racing contests. The women and girls spent most of their time cooking and serving.

The Pilgrims had so much to be thankful for. The long, hard, terrible year was over.

They gave thanks for good friends, new homes, and plenty of food. They gave thanks for the new life they had begun in Plymouth.